ONCE UPON A TIME

The 12 Days of Christmas in STORY and FILM

ONCE UPON A TIME

The 12 Days of Christmas in STORY and FILM

BRUCE G. EPPERLY

Anamchara Books

© 2024, Bruce G. Epperly

Anamchara Books
Vestal, New York 13850
www.AnamcharaBooks.com

All rights reserved. No part of this publication may be reproduced or transmitted for commercial purposes, except for brief quotations, without written permission of the publisher. Churches and other noncommercial interests may reproduce portions of this book without the express written permission of Anamchara Books, provided that the text does not exceed 500 words or 5 percent of the entire book, whichever is less, and that the text is not material quoted from another publisher. When reproducing text from this book, include the following credit line: "From *Once Upon a Time: The Twelve Days of Christmas in Story and Film* by Bruce G. Epperly, published by Anamchara Books. Used by permission."

Throughout this text, the author has chosen to paraphrase certain texts to honor the diversity of gender and sexual expression as representative of the all-embracing incarnational spirit of Christmas. Bible quotations are from the New Revised Standard Version Bible, copyright © 1989 National Council of the Churches of Christ in the United States of America. Used by permission. All rights reserved worldwide.

References to and the image representing "the Grinch" used in this book for the Tenth Day of Christmas material are based on the Dr. Seuss Enterprises' book, *How the Grinch Stole Christmas!* © 1985.

Paperback ISBN: 978-1-62524-919-7
eBook ISBN: 978-1-62524-920-3

CONTENTS

Once Upon a Time	7
From Cosmos to Cradle	17
Reading the Light, Seeing the Light, Being the Light	23

The Twelve Days of Christmas

Christmas Eve, December 24	29
Day 1: *Christmas Day, December 25*	33
Day 2: *December 26*	39
Day 3: *December 27*	47
Day 4: *December 28*	53
Day 5: *The Massacre of the Children, December 29*	59
Day 6: *December 30*	65
Day 7: *December 31*	71
Day 8: *January 1*	77
Day 9: *January 2*	81
Day 10: *January 3*	87
Day 11: *January 4*	91
Day 12: *January 5*	97
The Feast of Epiphany, January 6	103
Notes	109

ONCE UPON A TIME

Now the birth of Jesus the Messiah
took place in this way.
When his mother Mary had
been engaged to Joseph,
but before they lived together,
she was found to be pregnant
from the Holy Spirit.

(Matthew 1:18)

The beginning of
the good news
of Jesus Christ.

(Mark 1:1)

> God made humans because
> God loves stories.
>
> (Elie Wiesel)

This past Christmas season, I made the holiday's many stories my contemplative focal point. My goal was to experience the living God in all the Divine's many disguises and manifestations. I wanted to read, see, and be God's light in the Christmas season and all year round. And so, for fourteen days, beginning on Christmas Eve 2023 and concluding on the Feast of Epiphany 2024, I reflected on the stories of Jesus' birth in tandem with literature and media. This book is the fruit of those two weeks of reflection. It is my invitation to you to join me for fourteen days of insight and inspiration.

"Once upon a time": So begins many a good story. With the first lines of a story or introductory credits of a film, we embark on an adventure, indeed, often a heroic journey, with no clear destination and many twists and turns along the way. We may imagine a promised land, the far horizon, finding true love, or some great cause, and yet we must walk through the valley of the shadow of death, facing our own inner demons as well as dangers lurking in the darkness, before we can arrive at our destination.

The outcome of the journey is uncertain like our own lives, and we choose our own adventures as we witness the adventures of the characters, whether the storyline involves a mystery; meeting a true love; making peace with the past, family of origin, or an estranged friend; or discovering our authentic calling. And even as we read about others' adventures, we find ourselves on our own adventures of spiritual growth, personal sacrifice, and self-discovery. We come to realize that a good story or film is more than meets the eye. With J. R. R. Tolkein's heroic adventurers, we discover: "All that is gold does not glitter. Not all who wander are lost."

The deepest meanings are often hidden from those who try to shape the story to fit their own images of God. The story of Christmas, as Mark says, is "gospel" or "good news" for everyone, most especially the marginalized, forgotten, oppressed, elder, and young, who discover that in the challenges of life, God is with us, all of us, without exception.

A captivating book, poem, story, play, or film awakens our spirits and orients our lives. It can invite us to embark on a holy adventure with the often-anonymous God as our companion and fellow pilgrim. Indeed, God—the Source of Adventure and our Spiritual Home—is most often disguised within the ordinary moments of our lives. Only when we have arrived at our destination, do we discover

God's vision at work, and then we often find that the end of one good story inspires another pilgrimage. God is both companion and storyteller as our own lives unfold.

Since the early years of my childhood, reading has been the heart of my life and a portal into my own holy adventures. My earliest memories involve getting up at dawn to read with my father, while my brother and mother were still asleep. The early morning was my time with Dad before I went to school, and he sojourned to the Baptist church where he pastored. We read sports books, adventure stories, and mysteries. One of my fondest memories involves waking up to read John Steinbeck's *Travels with Charley,* which chronicles Steinbeck's ten-thousand-mile trip across the United States, accompanied by his standard poodle Charley. As a ten-year-old small-town boy, I couldn't wait to get up each morning to hear the accounts of interesting encounters, strange towns, and fascinating people. Steinbeck inspired me to become an intellectual vagabond long before I hit the road on my own pilgrimages.

I also dreamed of a career in professional baseball as I voraciously read most of the twenty-seven Bronc Burnett baseball and football books. Then, as a budding ten-year-old detective, I read dozens of Franklin Dixon's Hardy Boys mysteries. (Two decades later, I read them again to my son, and five decades later, to my grandsons.) An aficionado of mysteries, I journeyed with Sherlock Holmes and Dr. Watson on their adventures. (More recently, my grandsons and I have watched Sherlock's film interpretations, joining word and image seamlessly to bring new insights.)

Books, films, and stories still widen my circle of concern and curiosity. Reading also brings our family together for learning and sharing. When my middle school grandchildren are assigned a book for school, I buy my own copy of the book and read along with them. I can then discuss the book with them to discern deeper meanings. Reading opened me to the big world of other cultures and religions, and now I want to share those journeys with them.

And then there are the Christmas stories embedded in my spiritual and intellectual DNA. My father, a small-town Baptist pastor, had a special place in his heart for Henry van Dyke's *The Story of the Other Wiseman*. Each Christmas, we read the story as a family, and I have continued this practice with my own family for over forty years. I hope someday my grands may share the book, along with the Hardy Boys and Sherlock Holmes, with their own children; I may even live long enough to read these same stories with my great-grandchildren. We are making memories and writing our own stories with each turn of the page.

Christmas is the season of stories. During the Christmas season, we are invited into the adventures—and trials—of a teenage mother, unexpected father, lowly shepherds, and regal magi. We feel the love of Mary and Joseph for their child as well as the burdens of the journey to Bethlehem and the flight to Egypt. We discover angels in the most unexpected places, visiting a teenage girl, appearing in a dream to an uncertain father, singing "Hallelujah!" to shepherds, and warning the magi and holy family of danger ahead.

Although "all is calm and all is bright," we shudder as we catch a glimpse of Herod, overhear his interrogation of the magi, and then witness his terrible proclamation that the Child must be eliminated. We discover that baby Jesus is present as every newborn child at risk, whether through war, famine, household violence, poverty, or the machinations of power-hungry political leaders. Jesus' face is revealed in every immigrant child whose parents, like Mary and Joseph, are seeking asylum in a foreign land. As I listen to the morning news on NPR or see film footage of children on the U.S. borderlands, Sudan, Israel, Ukraine, or Gaza, I know that the massacre of the infants, perpetrated by heartless and calculating political leaders, is a reality today; I weep in solidarity with innocent suffering then and now.

My heart is broken when tyrants and political strong men demonize immigrants as "thugs," "rapists," and "vermin" who poison the purity of our nation. These same politicians blithely justify the murder of innocent children, separating children from their parents, and rounding up political opponents to ensure "national security" and their privileged way of life.

The Christmas story reminds us that we can orient our lives in better ways. In a world of chaos, violence, and hardheartedness, the Scrooge in us can make way for generosity and the Grinch who envies the happiness of others can experience a heart transplant! Celtic spiritual guide Pelagius proclaimed that every child comes into the world bearing the face of God—and as we meditate on the Christmas stories, whether written or on the screen, we realize the reality of that statement.

Told in the Gospels of Matthew, Luke, and John, the Christmas stories are "thin places" where time and eternity meet. These stories don't give us doctrines or rules; instead, they reveal God's vision for birth in our world of conflict and chaos and love and courage. They give us images and visions of God incarnate in a baby, the love of parents, and strangers following a star. They tell us that the Word of God becomes flesh right where we are in a body like ours, and each moment of life is a portal into God's heart. The Christmas stories awaken us to the incarnate God wrapped in human skin.

"God is with us," proclaim the angels. "Peace on earth, good will to all": That is the polestar of all human adventures. More than that, God is also *in* us, as near as our next breath—and God is in the stranger, those individuals we presume foes and adversaries, including family members from whom we may be alienated, as well as people with politics and policies that we challenge.

Through the Christmas narratives, God beckons us forward to face courageously and compassionately our daily challenges. Insightful stories and films remind us, as Howard Thurman avers, that we must always make room for the angels. There is hope, joy, and possibility even in the most dire-seeming circumstances.

The tales of Christmas in film and literature remind us that deep down, we all need spiritual healing: We are Scrooge and the Grinch, who must discover that life's meaning is found in generosity. We are Artaban, the other wise man, who fails in his intended journey to give homage to the Christ Child and finds God in the flesh of strangers on the way. We are George Bailey, who discovers that despite the chaos and challenges of family life and running a business, he has a wonderful life. We are the young couple who give their most precious possessions to bring joy to each other in "The Gift of the Magi." We are more than we can imagine when we open our hearts to the Divine in ourselves and others. Touched by God's loving companionship, we move from scarcity to abundance and self-interest to world loyalty. We become the magi, shepherds, and protective elders of our world.

In *The Gates of the Forest,* Elie Wiesel describes legendary Hasidic leaders who initially followed a clearly articulated ritual to achieve miracles to save their communities—but over time, they forget the prescribed words and actions. Still, even then, the rabbis can confess, "All I can do is tell the story." In the telling of ancient stories, the miracle of healing and salvation occurs. Long after we have forgotten the liturgies, doctrines, and rituals, the stories will sustain us. Truly, as Wiesel avers, "God made humans because God loves stories."

Remembering and sharing the stories of our faith is our calling as spiritual seekers and persons of faith. This is especially true in a time when doctrine is suspect; authentic relationship with God has been eclipsed by self-interest, political manipulation, and the love of power; and humanity is at risk due to the misuse of our technology and the impact of our industrial successes. Even now, we can recite the stories of a humble family, a star in the sky, angelic visitors, strangers from another religion, and shepherds in the field—and find that our hearts, heads, and hands are opened, and we are ready to face the future with hope.

Perhaps, we too will come to incarnate the miracles we need: changed hearts in our leaders and ourselves, a commitment to protect every newborn Christ Child, and the expansion of our focus from self-interest to world loyalty. Inspired by this ancient story and its power to change lives, we begin our journey through scripture, film, and story with a simple prayer hymn of Phillips Brooks.

> *O holy child of Bethlehem,*
> *Cast out our sin, and enter in,*
> *Be born in us today.*
> *We hear the Christmas angels,*
> *The great glad tidings tell,*
> *O Come to us, abide with us,*
> *Our Lord, Emmanuel.*

FROM COSMOS
TO CRADLE

In the beginning was the Word, and the
Word was with God, and the Word was God.
The Word was in the beginning with God.
All things came into being through
the Word, and without it not one thing
came into being. What has come into
being in God's Word was life, and
the life was the light of all people.

> The light shines in the darkness, and the
> darkness did not overtake it....
> And the Word became flesh and
> lived among us, and we have seen the
> Word's glory, the glory as of a parent's
> only child, full of grace and truth.
>
> (John 1:1–5,14)

> Love God in the world of the flesh.
>
> (W.H. Auden)

Four centuries before the birth of Jesus, the Greek philosopher Plato described time as the moving image of eternity. Celtic spirituality today speaks of a similar reality, thin places where the Infinite and Finite, Time and Eternity meet. Reaching beyond institutional Christianity, the Christmas story is universal as a revelation of holiness and beauty in the world of the flesh. In Bethlehem, West and East meet, and the light shines everywhere and in everyone. Our bodies are God's temple, and our spirits soar to the stars. Bethlehem's stable is everywhere, and every newborn has God's face. You were born wearing the face of Divinity—and it is still yours to wear today.

The Christmas stories join the cosmic adventure with our daily lives. The creative love and wisdom of God are embodied in a little child—and the little child leads us to experience the Christ within us and everyone. The Word and Wisdom of God, Logos and Sophia, that created the universe 13.7 billion years ago still brings forth, and still gives birth, to a Living Word in space and time, dwelling among us and within us.

The darkness cannot conquer God's everlasting light. Although bombs drop in the Middle East, immigrants, like Mary and Joseph, seek asylum, and parents grieve the loss of a child to illness or accident, Christmas reminds us that joy persists even in the bleakest nights. Christmas awakens us to the moral and spiritual arcs moving through history and our own lives, calling us to welcome the Christ Child in all of their many and often surprising disguises.

God's word comes to us in film, fiction, and scripture. "Once upon a time" joins yesterday, today, and tomorrow in an everlasting *now*. The stories of the Bethlehem Child, Scrooge, the Grinch, and even Rudolph, a "different" reindeer whose unique gifts guide Santa's way, awaken us to transform our own stories and the world. When we read ancient scripture, we discover our kinship with the biblical characters of the first Christmas story: We are also a young girl who discovers her amazing vocation, and we are that young man who chooses love rather than the dictates of his culture (even if it means humiliation). We might imagine we are an unnamed woman in a stable who midwives the birth of Jesus, for we are, as Meister Eckhart says, the midwives of God in our time. We are the Holy Family seeking asylum in Egypt, and we are refugees looking for a place to call home; we are workers in the fields suddenly overwhelmed by angelic voices, and we are pilgrims following a star.

In the telling and hearing of stories, whether we are young or old, we find the path to Bethlehem. The Word descends from Heaven to Earth, becomes flesh among us, and inspires us to share the good news that God is here for everyone. Our hearts are warmed, grow three sizes, and sacrifice becomes a joy, not a burden. We realize we truly have a wonderful life, and we can find miracles on every street corner as we experience the Christ Child as our intimate companion. In the spirit of the Advent oratorio, *For the Time Being*, we launch on a journey of adventure.

He is the Way.
Follow Him through the land of Unlikeness;
You will see rare beasts,
and have unique adventures.
He is the Truth.
Seek Him in the Kingdom of Anxiety;
You will come to a great city
that has expected your return for years.
He is the Life.
Love Him in the World of the Flesh.

(W. H. Auden)

READING THE LIGHT, SEEING THE LIGHT, BEING THE LIGHT

The true light, which enlightens everyone was coming into the world.

(John 1:9)

You are the light of
the world....
Let your light shine.

(Matthew 5:14,16)

Do not be conformed
to this world,
but be transformed by the
renewing of your mind,
so that you may discern
God's vision—
what is good and
acceptable and perfect.

(Romans 12:2–3)

Spiritual guides counsel us to contemplate or meditate upon the stories of scripture so that they become *our* stories. In so doing, we shape our lives according to scripture. Insightful scholars also counsel that God comes to us in the stories of other faith traditions and in literature and art often described as secular. With every word, God is birthed into our lives, and our spirits are enlightened and enlivened. All reading can be holy reading (*lectio divina*) in which we receive Divine inspiration whenever we pick up a book.

When we see the light of God in these stories, we recognize that we are also the light of God in the world. The light in Bethlehem becomes our light, and we share the light with others. We hear the voices of angels, turn to the better angels in ourselves, and become angels ourselves, messengers of the Holy to others.

The philosopher Alfred North Whitehead, whose insights have shaped my understanding of Christianity, asserts:

> The essence of Christianity is the appeal to the life of Christ as a revelation of the nature of God and of his agency in the world . . . there can be no doubt as to what elements in the record have evoked a response from all that is best in human

nature. The Mother, the Child, and the bare manger: the lowly man, homeless and self-forgetful, with his message of peace, love, and sympathy: the suffering, the agony, the tender words as life ebbed, the final despair: and the whole with the authority of supreme victory.[1]

Whitehead asserts that the great tragedy of Christian history is that Christians have often substituted the love of power for the power of love and worshipped abstract doctrines instead of the concrete living and loving God of flesh and blood. In that false worship, we have often followed the way of Caesar to the neglect of Jesus' message of peace and hospitality. Whitehead also says:

> There is, however, in the Galilean origin of Christianity yet another suggestion. . . . It does not emphasize the ruling Caesar, or the ruthless moralist, or the unmoved mover. It dwells upon the tender elements in the world, which slowly and in quietness operate by love; and it finds purpose in the present immediacy of a kingdom not of this world.[2]

In reading the Christmas stories, we discover that the simple Galilean origins of Christian faith are not the quest for theological, ecclesiastical, or political control but rather the heart of our spiritual adventure. I believe that the sacred permeates the secular and the secular reveals the sacred. Accordingly, we can find God in a story, novel, film, play, and poem as well as in carols and scriptures. Stories and films, along with scriptures, can open our hearts and expand our spirits. We can find gospel inspiration in the scriptures and also in a good book, short story, or film.

In the course of my Christmas contemplations, I followed a particular spiritual practice to deepen my experience of the days of Christmas, from Christmas Eve through the Feast of Epiphany, January 6th. You may choose to follow this practice—or you might choose one that best suits your personality, faith, and lifestyle. Just as there are many ways to experience the Divine, there are many paths to deepen your Christmas spirituality.

Christmas is a season, not just one day; in fact, it is a lifetime. As you live the twelve days of Christmas in companionship with the Christ Child, you will experience every day—and all year long—as Christmas Day, a celebration of life in which the child in you and the Child of God join hands in the wondrous dance of God's love.

CHRISTMAS PRACTICE

Here is a simple way to see, be, and share the light of the Christ Child as you read this book. With a flexible spirit:

1. Begin with a time of silence, asking the Christ Child to be born in your life.

2. Read the scripture at the beginning of each day's reading.

3. Slowly read that day's meditation. You are not reading for entertainment or knowledge; you are reading as a form of prayer. Open your heart to hearing God's voice speaking to you through the written words.

4. Then read the scripture again. Pause to meditate on the words. Take a few minutes to sit in silence, letting the words of the quotations soak into your mind. Note any insights and inspirations.

5. Read the rest of that day's "Christmas Practice." Spend some time journaling and/or praying as you consider the questions I've asked.

6. Commit to being alert today, ready to follow the way of Jesus in every encounter.

7. Conclude with the prayer I've given at the end of each day's reading.

8. When you are tempted to lose the Christmas spirit in anxiety, anger, or apathy, call yourself back to the theme of the day, without judgment or guilt.

9. If time permits during your day, you might read one of the stories or a film highlighted on a particular day's reflection.

A CHRISTMAS PRAYER

This year, may the Christ Child be born in me.
May I see Christ everywhere
and be a messenger of the Christ Child to everyone.
May I live by Tiny Tim's blessing:
"God bless us, everyone."

CHRISTMAS EVE

DECEMBER 24

The angel said, "Do not be afraid, Mary,
for you have found favor with God...."
Then Mary said, "Here am I,
the servant of the Lord;
let it be with me according to your word."

(Luke 1:30,38)

In one of my earliest Christmas Eve memories, our family gathers around their newly purchased Zenith black-and-white television to watch *Amahl and the Night Visitors*. I believe it was 1957 when I first saw Gian Carlo Menotti's opera, depicting the encounter of a young boy, his mother, and the three magi. A child with disabilities, living in poverty and forced to beg for daily bread, Amahl's imagination is not yet quenched, despite his mother's fears that he will be a beggar for life.

To their astonishment, Amahl and his mother receive three strange visitors, wealthy yet weary. Though they have little to offer their royal guests, Amahl and his mother shelter them for the night. During the night, Amahl's desperate mother steals some of the gold intended for the Christ Child. When she is apprehended by the magi's page, Amahl rises to her defense. His mother confesses that she has waited a lifetime for the coming of a king whose love would embrace the poor and persons with disabilities; she gives back the gold to the magi. In gratitude for their mercy, she wants to make a gift to the Child King but has nothing to offer. Overcome with emotion, Amahl offers his crutch, and that act of kindness leads to his leg being miraculously healed. With his mother's permission, Amahl joins the magi, taking his one gift, his crutch, to give the Child of Bethlehem.

Christmas is still the season of strange guests and impossible possibilities. Angels visit Mary and Joseph, presenting them with a vision of God in us and with us to transform the world. The angelic message and God's message to us is, again and again: "Do not be afraid." The task before you, like that of Mary and Joseph, may be impossible, according to any rational calculus, and yet the world depends on your response. Bravely, Mary and Joseph embrace the impossible themselves, not knowing what it will mean for them and the child. They say "yes." Upon that "yes," theirs and ours, the world depends.

At Christmas, God is with us calling us beyond our wildest dreams, to launch out into the deep, like the Celtic spiritual guides who embarked on sea voyages in rudderless boats called coracles. God says, "Do not be afraid," for when Divinity calls us to new adventures in strange lands, the Divine also prepares, guides, protects, and gives us the courage to say "yes" to the adventure ahead, one step at a time.

A young peasant girl, with no social position, says "yes" to the Divine—despite the risks of an unexpected, out-of-wedlock pregnancy. That "yes" changes history. It challenges us to also say "yes" in our time.

TODAY'S CHRISTMAS PRACTICE

Read Luke 1:30, 38 again, slowly and prayerfully. Now, take a moment to imagine yourself in Mary's place as

she is visited by an angel. What message might the angel have for you? What is waiting to be born in you? How might you make way for Jesus' birth in our world today?

To what great work is God calling you? Each of us is essential to the Realm of Heaven; each of us has our unique role to play. What is your role? Do you know? If not, pray that the Holy One will reveal this to you.

Every great work begins with a small step, taken on faith, despite our misgivings. When we say "yes," the world opens up. We can embody the words of Phillips Brooks: "O holy Child of Bethlehem, descend to us we, pray; cast out our sin, and enter in; be born in us today. . . . O come to us, abide with us, Our Lord, Emmanuel."

A CHRISTMAS PRAYER

Awaken me to the voices of angels.
Awaken me to your call in every millisecond
that I might be a midwife of Incarnation in my life,
the lives of those around me, and in the world.

CHRISTMAS DAY

DECEMBER 25

> And she gave birth to her firstborn son and wrapped him in bands of cloth and laid him in a manger, because there was no place in the guest room.
>
> (Luke 2:7)

I first saw *A Charlie Brown Christmas* in 1965. I was thirteen and struggling to find a spiritual path. Due to a faith-related trauma, I no longer felt comfortable in the church of my childhood. In fact, I felt claustrophobic, as though a narrow and pain-filled faith had constricted my spirit as well as my lungs. But that Christmas, as I sat transfixed before our Zenith television, watching Charlie, Lucy, Linus, Snoopy, and their friends trying to find Christmas, I felt a glimmer of the Christmas message. This was different from the one expressed by the conservative faith of my childhood, a fresh take that gave me a sense of hope and possibility.

Charlie Brown loves Christmas, but this year, he feels depressed, unable to get in the spirit; he is troubled by the commercialization of Jesus' birth. The ever-wise Lucy tells him he should buy a tree and direct the children's Christmas play. Charlie's play-directing debut falls into chaos, however, and his Christmas tree, the scrawniest in the yard, inspires ridicule among his friends.

Then, when Charlie exclaims, "Isn't there anyone who can tell me what Christmas is all about?" Linus steps forward and recites the angelic annunciation to the shepherds. "That is what Christmas is all about," Linus proclaims. Charlie's Christmas spirit is salvaged when his friends decorate his tiny Christmas tree and discover it truly is beautiful. Charlie and his friends discover that Christmas is not about presents and purchases. Instead, the true Christmas spirit finds meaning in the most unexpected places and in the lives of the most unexpected people. Christmas, it turns out, is about God's gifts to us and our gifts to one another.

Many of us struggle to experience the Christmas spirit—and with good reason. Too many people are alone at Christmas. Family may be far away or ruptured, and reconciliation seems impossible. Or there's an empty place at the table, making the holiday feel strange and lonely. Perhaps, the commercial Christmas leaves us cold, but a literal and unimaginative reading of the Christmas story no longer fits into our worldview. The faith of our early years, the closeness we may have felt to the Divine, is gone (and often for good reason when theological doctrines tell us that we're sinners bound for hell because of past deeds, doubt, or sexual identity).

Mary and Joseph were also outsiders in many ways. The challenges they faced were an unplanned pregnancy, economic distress, and an oppressive government that forced them to travel at Mary's most vulnerable time in order to pay a tax. Worse yet, they couldn't find a place for the child to be born. They had to depend on the kindness of strangers to find a rough-hewn birthplace for Jesus. Powerful occupying forces determined their lives

Luke's story of Jesus' birth is anything but romantic. There are no celebrations or family get-togethers—just a family without shelter. Bethlehem is a small community of no consequence to the larger political and social scenes—

and yet out of backwater Bethlehem comes the Light of the World, the birth upon which the future of the world hinges. Amid anxiety, uncertainty, danger, and even simple, ordinary life, God shows up.

When there is no room in the inn, God has room. When disappointment and alienation rupture our lives, the Spirit enters to mend and build bridges. Where we feel lost with no spiritual GPS, Divinity leads us to the unadorned and often unpretentious presence of new life. Hope is reborn, and a way is made. Once more, let us look to Phillips Brooks' hymn for a reminder of the illumination that glows in the places where life is dim, when we feel alone without direction or a home base: "Yet in your dark streets shineth the everlasting light; the hopes and fears of all the years are met in thee tonight."

TODAY'S CHRISTMAS PRACTICE

Pause awhile now to read meditatively Luke 2:1–20. May your heart be awakened to the challenges faced by Mary and Joseph, the birth of Jesus, and the angelic announcement to the shepherds. Imagine if you had been there, with the shepherds on their hillside or with Mary and Joseph as Mary labors through the night to deliver her baby. What do you feel? What draws your attention? What lessons do the shepherds have to teach you? What wisdom do Mary and Joseph impart to you?

A CHRISTMAS PRAYER

O Houseless Baby Jesus, let me see you
in all of your distressing and alienating disguises.
Let me see you in the lost, lonely, and forgotten
as well as my beloved kin.
Let your face shine in every undocumented worker,
asylum seeker, and houseless person,
as well as my loved ones.
Let me hear your voice in the cries of every baby
and the laughter of every child, knowing
that each family is a holy family
and every child comes to earth bearing your divinity.
Let my heart be broken
by the reality of homelessness,
hunger, and inadequate health care.
Let me be your welcome arms to every seeking soul,
to every lost child and prevaricating politician.
Let me see your face in every newborn
—and in every toddler, teenager, adult, and elder.
Be born in my heart and in the world today.

THE SECOND DAY OF CHRISTMAS

DECEMBER 26

Now in that same region there were shepherds living in the fields, keeping watch over their flock by night. Then an angel of the Lord stood before them, and the glory of the Lord shone around them, and they were terrified. But the angel said to them, "Do not be afraid, for see, I am bringing you good news of great joy for all the people: to you is born this day in the city of David a Savior, who is the Messiah, the Lord.

(Luke 2:9–11)

Frank Capra's *It's a Wonderful Life* is one of the staples of our family's yearly Christmas celebration. I suspect I have seen the Capra film, featuring Jimmy Stewart and Donna Reed, three dozen times over the years. George Bailey, overcome with disappointment, despair, and dejection about the roads not taken and the hopes unrealized, contemplates suicide. Just as he is about to jump to his death, he is saved by an angelic visitation: a bumbling angel named Clarence, who needs just one success to get his wings.

Clarence presents George with a life review, challenging him to see his life from a broader perspective. He asks George to ponder what would have happened if he hadn't been born. If George had never lived, his brother would have drowned and never become a war hero, the local pharmacist would have accidentally killed a patient, the town would be in shambles and at the mercy of a predatory businessman, and George's wife would never have found love.

That's the "George Bailey Principle." It teaches us that we emerge from and contribute to the intricate interdependence of life in which each of us matters. It's very similar to the African wisdom expressed by *Ubuntu*: "I am because of you; we are because of one another." The world is saved one moment and action at a time, and each of us is a potential savior of the world. Each action can be a tipping point from darkness to light and death to life. We make a difference in the lives of the people we meet and the world in which we live.

Economics plays a major role in the stories of Jesus' birth. We see the contrast between the wealth and power of Herod and his minions—and the poverty and powerlessness of the shepherds. Houseless and at the bottom of the economic ladder, shepherds were nevertheless necessary to the Judean economy. Like the undocumented workers picking our vegetables and fruit, working at packing plants, and taking care of our elders, self-important people looked down upon the shepherds, mistrusted them, and harassed them—even though shepherds were "essential workers" necessary to the region's economy. God comes to these oppressed and overlooked people; they, not the religious and political elite, receive the revelation of the Christ Child.

Divinity is always revealed in the "least of these." Ostracized and manipulated by others, the shepherds are forever changed that Christmas Eve. God shows them they are beloved; they matter; they have a role in the story of salvation. I suspect their economic and social situation did not change, certainly not immediately, but they received a new sense of identity. Carrying God's affirmation with them in the years ahead, the unrecorded stories of their lives must surely have been illuminated by that single night when they heard the angels sing.

As Howard Thurman says:

> There must be always remaining in every [person]'s life some place for the singing of the angels—someplace for that which in itself is breathlessly beautiful and by an inherent prerogative throwing all the rest of life into a new and created relatedness. Something that gathers up into itself all the freshets of experience from drab and commonplace areas of living and glows in one bright light of penetrating beauty and meaning. . . .

The commonplace is shot through now with new glory—old burdens become lighter, deep and ancient wounds lose much of their old, old hurting. A crown is placed over our heads that for the rest of our lives we are trying to grow tall enough to wear. Despite all the crassness of life, despite all the harshness of life, life is saved by the singing of angels.

In earlier times, people believed that angels were our co-workers as we seek to build the Realm of God. Now, in ways we can't imagine, the angels still need us, and we need them. They need us—and God needs us—to be their companions in healing the world. We add to the angelic presence in our world when we say "yes" to God, "yes" to love, "yes" to one another.

TODAY'S CHRISTMAS PRACTICE

Pause awhile to again read Luke 2:8–20. Take a moment to ponder how the angelic vision may have changed the shepherds' lives. Where have you (or where might you) encounter an angel? How would your life be changed? Would it change the way you think? The way you act?

God loves you. You too matter to the story of the world's salvation. You too can do something beautiful for God. You too can work with the angels to bring love and justice to this world. It truly is a wonderful life.

And so, on this second day of Christmas, let us listen, with the shepherds, for the singing of the angels.

A CHRISTMAS PRAYER

When I confront strangers and challenges,
remind me, Life Giver,
to listen for the angels' message:
"Do not be afraid."
Give me ears to hear angelic melodies
interwoven with today's ordinary noises.
May I, like the shepherds,
run to Bethlehem to see the Christ Child.
Let me race to love, race to heal,
and race to share the Good News of great joy:
God's peace on Earth and goodwill to all.

THE THIRD DAY OF CHRISTMAS

DECEMBER 27

> But Mary treasured all these words and pondered them in her heart.
>
> (Luke 2:19)

We are children of memory and hope. Truman Capote's short story "A Christmas Memory" chronicles one Christmas in the life of seven-year-old "Buddy" and his sixty-something cousin, who's known to her family and community as an eccentric not fully of this world. Every Christmas, Buddy and his cousin gather up all the money they've saved in the previous year to make fruitcakes to give away to friends, people they've met during the year, and even President Truman.

In the chill of pre-Christmas autumn, the anticipated day arrives; Buddy's elder cousin proclaims, "It's fruitcake weather." The two of them go to work buying supplies, including bootlegged whiskey, to make at least thirty fruitcakes. The joy is in the making, the camaraderie, and the giving. In those innocent moments, memories are made that last a lifetime. What delight it is to send off the last fruitcake! They wonder: Will Mrs. Truman serve it at Christmas breakfast this year?

When Christmas finally comes, Buddy and his cousin, with little money left, give each other inexpensive gifts: kites. As the wind picks up, off they go to send their kites heavenward in playful celebration.

As she looks at the sky, Buddy's cousin discovers:

> You know what I've always thought. . . I've always thought a body would have to be sick and dying before they saw the Lord. And I imagined that when He came it would be like looking at the Baptist window: pretty as colored glass with the sun pouring through, such a shine you don't know it's getting dark. And it's been a comfort: to think of that shine taking away all the spooky feeling. But I'll wager it never happens. I'll wager at

the very end a body realizes the Lord has already shown Himself. That things as they are just what they've always seen, was seeing Him. As for me, I could leave the world with today in my eyes.

That moment of epiphany when Heaven and Earth meet marks their last Christmas together. Buddy's family sends him to military school to put him on the "right path." Although they never see each other again, Buddy and his cousin continue to communicate—she sends him the best fruitcake every Christmas!—until she falls into decrepitude and dementia.

A few years later, Buddy hears news of her death.

And when that happens, I know it. A message saying so merely confirms a piece of news some secret vein had already received, severing me from an irreplaceable part of myself, letting it loose like a kite on a broken string. That is why, walking across a school campus on this particular December morning, I keep searching the sky. As if I expected to see, rather like hearts, a lost pair of kites hurrying towards heaven.

Even small events can reveal the heart of the Universe. And they continue to shape and influence our lives, for God comes to us in memory and hope. When we open our spiritual eyes, we can, as William Blake says, see the world as it is: infinite.

Some moments define our lifetimes. Christmas memories can shine a light on the rest of our lives. The heavens open up, and we see "a pair of kites hurrying towards heaven."

I remember the birth of our son, that first cry, and holding him in my arms for the first time. I remember being filled to the brim with a love that was bigger than me; I have tried ever since, all my life, to live up to that love. I also remember the births of our grandsons and the deaths of my parents, brother, and closest friend; these were all holy moments, chockful with God's presence. Each time, I stood on holy ground with myriad angels all around. Truly Divinity was in these places, and I glimpse it as I treasure these memories each day.

Scripture suggests that Mary had several other children—at least six—and each was treasured by their mother and bore God's holy light (see Matthew 12:48; 13:55). But on this particular night, surrounded by shepherds, angels, and friendly beasts, Divine light flooded her life, illuminating the rest of her days.

TODAY'S CHRISTMAS PRACTICE

Pause awhile now to reread Luke 2:19 slowly and prayerfully. Take a moment to imagine Mary treasuring that holy night when her baby Jesus was born, a moment in which Heaven and Earth met and the Word was made flesh.

In moments of selfless love and hospitality, we too give birth to Divinity. This verse from Luke's Gospel invites us also to ponder, like Mary, the moments when Christ is born in our lives. Moments when the light shines, and we are forever changed.

Spend some time recalling Christmases past. What memories still warm your heart? What experiences do you treasure, regardless of how long ago they occurred? How have those experiences changed you? How do they still shape your life? How might you make more room for their light to continue to illuminate your thoughts and actions? How do these moments invite you to live fully and energetically today, making each day a Christmas?

Each day, every moment, is an opportunity for the holy to be born once more in your life. Tonight, as you go to bed, think back on the day. Notice the moments when the Christ Child emerged from the day's ordinary events.

A CHRISTMAS PRAYER

Let me remember, God of the Past,
the joys of Christmas past.
Let me delight in moments of grace and wonder,
in generosity and love, and let Christmas present
be filled with possibility, adventure, welcome,
and gratitude for the One Made Flesh
in pies and candy, hugs and mistletoe,
renewed friendships,
and the simple delight of children and the child in me.

THE FOURTH DAY OF CHRISTMAS

DECEMBER 28

An angel of the Lord appeared
to him in a dream
and said, "Joseph, son of
David, do not be afraid
to take Mary as your wife,
for the child conceived in her
is from the Holy Spirit."

(Matthew 1:20)

> An angel of the Lord appeared
> to Joseph in a dream
> and said, "Get up, take the child and
> his mother, and flee to Egypt."
>
> (Matthew 2:13)

In *Probity Jones and the Fear Not Angel,* Walter Wangerin describes the Christmas adventures of a pre-teen city girl. When she gets sick, she is unable to attend the Christmas Pageant in which she was to play the part of the Fear Not Angel, the best part she'd ever had. Convalescing on the living room sofa, Probity hears an insistent knock. When she opens the door, a beautiful dark-skinned angel takes her on a journey to Bethlehem. Whether as a result of her sickness, imagination, dream, or mystical experience, Probity Jones is transported back in time to the birth of Jesus

There, she is able to take part in another pageant; she is part of the angelic chorus led by the Fear Not Angel. The Fear Not Angel also gives her a gift, a shining shawl. When they return from the pageant, Probity exclaims to her amazed mother: "O, Mama, the angel gave me a piece of herself to keep forever and forever more."

The world is full of mystery, shot through with magic and miracle. I'm not making a claim for a separate, supernatural reality; I'm expressing my belief that our world, our bodies, and the events of our lives are all filled with Divinity. Quantum physicists tell us that the world we see and touch is not the "real world"; they point toward the existence of a far vaster, stranger Reality, where the very particles of the world are connected, interwoven, across space and time.

Twentieth-century psychologist Carl Jung believed the world is knit together by unseen forces. We glimpse these in dreams, intuitions, and synchronicities. We hear their echoes in our stories and myths. The Unseen World is all around us.

Like Jung, the Bible takes dreams seriously. Joseph listens to his dreams. Much like his spiritual ancestor, another dreamer, Joseph the son of Jacob, God speaks to Joseph of Nazareth in dreams. Worried about Mary's unexpected pregnancy and uncertain of what path to take, Joseph has a nocturnal visitor who reassures him the child is from God. "Fear not," the angel tells him. "Go ahead. Marry the girl. The world will be forever transformed. That child will be Emmanuel, God with us." Joseph lets go of his fears and follows angelic guidance.

Two more times, Joseph receives life-changing dreams, telling him to flee to Egypt and then return to Nazareth after the death of Herod. Perhaps these dreams inspired Joseph throughout his life, awakening his sensitivity to God's voice in times of crisis and decision-making.

God is constantly speaking to us, using a variety of media: scripture, mystical experiences, synchronous encounters, the book of Nature, the counsel of friends, and dreams. But do we listen? Or do we assume such moments are purely accidental, not worth our attention? Might they in fact be the Spirit whispering in "sighs too deep for words" (Romans 8:26)?

TODAY'S CHRISTMAS PRACTICE

Pause now to meditate on Matthew 1:8–25 and 2:13. Reflect on moments when God may have spoken to you in a dream or a synchronous encounter. Where else is God speaking to you? Are you listening? Take note of your dreams. You might even ask God to grant you dreams with spiritual insights to help you find your way in the chaos of our times. A journal can be a helpful tool for recording your dreams, daily spiritual experiences, and memorable moments. Take time throughout your day to reflect on these.

A CHRISTMAS PRAYER

When I am afraid, O God, send me your angels.
When I am uncertain, give me a dream.
When I am lonely, open my senses
to perceive the love around me.
When I feel powerless, give me imagination
and energy to be your companion
in healing the world one act at a time.

THE FIFTH DAY OF CHRISTMAS

The Massacre of the Children

DECEMBER 29[3]

Now after the magi had left, an angel of the Lord appeared to Joseph in a dream and said, "Get up, take the child and his mother, and flee to Egypt, and remain there until I tell you, for Herod is about to search for the child, to destroy him. Then Joseph got up, took the child and his mother by night, and went to Egypt and remained there until the death of Herod. This was to fulfill what had been spoken by the Lord through the prophet, "Out of Egypt I have called my son." When Herod saw that he had been tricked by the magi, he was infuriated, and he sent and killed all the children in and around Bethlehem who were two years old or under, according to the time that he had learned from the magi.

(Luke 2:13–17)

In his short story "Santa Claus is a White Man," Hunter University professor John Henrick Clarke describes the cultural and racial prejudice that infects a child's Christmas celebration with hate and suffering.[4] Tragically, when our Christmas symbols are misused to reflect our prejudices and privilege, they can hurt as well as heal and diminish as well as exalt. We can become insensitive to angelic voices and fixate on the demons of division. We can let our prejudice and hate shape our interpretation of this joyful holiday.

Clarke's tale is only too representative of racist Jim Crow America. When a mother, the servant of a wealthy white merchant, gives her son Randolph a quarter to buy

Christmas gifts, he is the "happiest little colored boy in all of Louisiana." Randolph's joy turns to terror and trauma, however, when on his way to buy presents, he is accosted by a group of angry white boys. Determined to put him "in his place," they threaten to lynch him. He seeks solace from Santa Claus, who confiscates his quarter and then tells the crowd that he's too small to be lynched. "Let's let 'im live awhile . . . maybe we'll get 'im later," Santa says and then gives the coin to the bully who threatened Randolph's life.

"Sure, there is a Santa Claus!" the bully exclaims as he pockets the coin.

When Randolph returns to his own neighborhood,

> he decided he would tell no one except his mother. She, perhaps, could understand, and either give him a new quarter or do his shopping for him. But, what would he say about that awful figure of a Santa Claus? There were some things no one, not even mothers, could explain.

Not all Christmas stories are pretty. Thanks to Joseph's dream, he and his family escape Herod's clutches—but not every family is so fortunate. Imagine the shock, horror, and sorrow we would feel if our government put to death every baby boy in the country! Mary and Joseph may have felt "survivors' guilt" when they realized their son survived while scores of children died as a result of Herod's quest to murder the Christ Child. Jesus' own sense of solidarity with those who suffer may even have first emerged when he heard stories about the massacre of infants.

In many ways, little has changed since Herod's cruel decree. God's incarnation takes place in a world of intentional oppression and violence, much of it the result of political decisions. Our leaders still make decisions that cause children to die. On our borders, toddlers were separated from their parents in detention camps; some of them failed to survive. Thousands of children die of starvation in Africa due to famine and civil war. The names Parkland, Columbine, Sandy Hook, and Uvalde (and too many others) reflect our elected legislators' choice to value assault-style weapons more than children's lives. As I write these words in December 2023, children are dying in Gaza, and parents mourn in Israel due to the violence of political leaders.

And amid all this violence, God calls us to be instruments of peace. We cannot be silent in the face of evil. We cannot let our feelings of helplessness and apathy hold us back. We must see every child as our child or grandchild, bearing the face of Christ and deserving our care. We work with the angels to bring the day when "they shall beat their swords into plowshares and their spears into pruning hooks; nation shall not lift up sword against nation; neither shall they learn war any more" (Isaiah 2:4).

TODAY'S CHRISTMAS PRACTICE

Reread Luke 2:13–17. What images and words jump out at you? Note that Joseph takes immediate action after he receives God's message. He does not dilly or dally, filled with self-doubt, as you or I might do, were we in that situation.

Have you ever felt a Divine call to a specific action or way of life? If so, how did you "hear" the call? If not, do you believe God can speak to you in that way? Are you willing to listen? Does anything in your life make it harder to hear the sacred Voice speaking your name?

When we consider the plight of the world's children, so often we feel helpless and hopeless. Ask the Holy One to show you one small action you can take today on behalf of these little ones (whether they are near or far).

A CHRISTMAS PRAYER

*In this Christmas season,
we are tempted to focus only on joyful experiences
and drown out the suffering of others
with our carols and consumerism.
We don't want to see the bombs lighting up the skies,
view immigrants at our nation's borders,
or witness people without shelter.
Wake us up, shake us up, Life Giver,
that we might see the tragic beauty of life,
and do whatever we can
to ease the pain and suffering of the world.
Show us specific actions we can take
to make the world a safer place for all children.
Let us be on the side of the angels,
bringing comfort and peace.
Let us be instruments of peace and reconciliation
in the name of the Christ Child.*

THE SIXTH DAY OF CHRISTMAS

DECEMBER 30

He has brought down the powerful from
their thrones
and lifted up the lowly;
he has filled the hungry with good things
and sent the rich away empty.

(Luke 1:52–53)

First published in 1844, Charles Dickens' *A Christmas Carol* is the quintessential Christmas tale of spiritual transformation. The name *Ebenezer Scrooge*, like *Grinch*, says everything about the main character. Indeed, "Scrooge" has become a catchall to describe anyone who is tight-fisted or pecuniary, whether in personal relationships or politics. Scrooges put profits above people and will do anything to increase their fortune. Dickens describes Ebenezer Scrooge in these words: "Scrooge! a squeezing, wrenching, grasping, scraping, clutching, covetous, old sinner . . . self-contained, and solitary as an oyster."

On a dreary Christmas Eve, seven years after the death of his business partner Jacob Marley, Ebenezer Scrooge glimpses Marley's face glaring at him from his door knocker. Then, in the course of the night, the old skinflint encounters the ghosts of Christmas past, present, and future. Each presents him with visions of his life: what was, what is now, and what is to come in the future. Scrooge's life review confronts the miser with the contrast between his hopeful youth and the shriveled, closed-hearted person he's become. He sees the pain he causes to his employee Bob Cratchit and his alienation from his good-hearted and gregarious nephew Fred. Scrooge realizes that Cratchit's son, Tiny Tim, will die without proper medical care. Looking toward his future, Scrooge envisions a lonely death, with no mourners, and a neglected grave with no visitors.

Scrooge pleads with the Ghost of Christmas Future for a different outcome and a changed life. "Before I draw nearer to that stone to which you point," says Scrooge, "answer me one question. Are these the shadows of the things that will be, or are they shadows of things that may be, only?" Scrooge continues, saying our "courses will foreshadow certain ends, to which, if persevered in, they must lead . . . but if the courses be departed from, the ends will change. Say it is thus with what you show me."

As he stands beside his own future grave, Scrooge vows:

> I will honour Christmas in my heart, and try to keep it all the year. I will live in the Past, the Present, and the Future. The Spirits of all Three shall strive within me. I will not shut out the lessons that they teach. Oh, tell me I may sponge away the writing on this stone!

Scrooge has been spiritually transformed. He awakens on Christmas morning a new person, generous, civic-minded, and kind to all. In the years ahead, he becomes Tiny Tim's "second father" and the epitome of what it means to celebrate Christmas. His life is a worthy expression of Tiny Tim's affirmation: "God bless us, every one."

An old saying advises us not to mix religion and politics; we want to be especially sensitive about this during the holidays and most certainly at the Christmas dinner table. At the same time, we want to speak words of truth and grace; we cannot "go along" with racist, misogynistic, or other hurtful conversations.

Mary, Jesus' mother, defines the prudent path between tact and truth. She is anything but meek and mild in the Magnificat, her hymn to God. As an expectant mother, she wants her child to grow up in a world in which he will have the opportunity to flourish—and that means radical economic change. She doesn't want him to be crushed by oppression, imperialism, and poverty. And so she sings an "impossible possibility" that's as dramatic as Gabriel's visitation.

Mary describes a world in which all people have food, homes, health care, education, and power, a world where the walls of economic and class separation are torn down forever. "Meek and mild" Mary prophesies a social revolution in which everyone belongs, everyone flourishes, and everyone joins hands in community.

TODAY'S CHRISTMAS PRACTICE

Read the full Magnificat (Luke 1:46–55). Then pause and prayerfully consider her words. Reflect on ways our society needs to change to ensure everyone has sufficient resources for an abundant life for themselves and their children.

How might you honor both the Christ Child and his mother by transforming our world today? How might you work with others to turn things upside down so they can finally be right side up? What can you do today to make God's realm come alive "on earth as it is in heaven" (Matthew 6:10)?

A CHRISTMAS PRAYER

Make me aware, Holy One,
each time you see me close my heart,
unwilling to reach out with love.
When I am ruled by fear or apathy,
wake me up to the truth of your love.
When all I see is scarcity,
show me that all around me is abundance.
Open my heart to give
from the many resources you have given me.
May I embrace the Spirit of Christmas
here and now—and in the future.
I want to be like the transformed Scrooge,
leaving a legacy of love wherever I go.

THE SEVENTH DAY OF CHRISTMAS

DECEMBER 31

Glory to God in the highest heaven,
and on earth peace among
those whom he favors!

(Luke 2:14)

On New Year's Eve, we need God's light to guide our path into the year ahead. Sometimes, the light comes from the most unexpected places!

I first encountered the story of Rudolph the Red-Nosed Reindeer in 1964 when I was a twelve-year-old. I knew the song about Rudolph, but now there was a television special based on his story. There was also a children's book, commissioned by Montgomery Ward some twenty years earlier.

I was a country kid who hadn't yet adjusted to life in the city of San Jose, California. I felt like a misfit trying to fit in with the more "cosmopolitan" and streetwise children of our neighborhood. When the other reindeer "wouldn't let poor Rudolph join in any reindeer games," I could identify with his situation,

We all know the story. As a result of his shiny nose, Rudolph doesn't fit in and is shunned—today, we would say bullied—by his fellow reindeer. Rudolph tries to hide his unique physical characteristic, but he is soon discovered and ostracized. Because his big red nose makes him look different from the other reindeer, they assume he must *be* different, deficient, and socially handicapped. Even Santa participates in the discrimination, shunning the "differently abled" Rudolph because of his red, shiny nose. The North Pole community, much like our own, sees uniformity as a sign of beauty and belonging.

Only when Christmas is jeopardized due to foggy weather is Rudolph seen for what he truly is—a unique, gifted, and necessary member of Santa's reindeer team. His "disability" saves the community! With his glowing nose to light the way, he makes Christmas possible after all.

Perhaps, writing the story was therapeutic for its author Robert May, who was a small, shy boy; he confessed he knew all too well what it was like to be an underdog. He wrote the story at a dark time in his life, after his wife's death. May recalled: "Spring slipped into summer. . . . I needed Rudolph now more than ever. Gratefully I buried myself in the writing." About a month later, before submitting the draft to Montgomery Ward, he read it to his daughter Barbara and his in-laws. "In their eyes I could see that the story accomplished what I had hoped." The darkness of depression, disability, and difference gave birth to a holy light.

"Glory to God in the highest!" sing the angels. "The whole earth is full of God's glory!" chant the angelic host when they confront Isaiah in the Jerusalem Temple. Beauty is everywhere—even where you least expect it to be found. Even in people who seem unlovable. You may be amazed! And, as Rabbi Abraham Joshua Heschel says, wonder and radical amazement are at the heart of religious experience.

Like Rudolph, the shepherds are outcasts in their society. But one dark night, they encounter God's messengers and hear the voices of heaven. Their souls and cells are transformed. Regardless of how other people regard them, they have learned their self-worth. Life will never be the same for them. From then on, I feel certain the shepherds sought to live up to God's love and unique care for them.

The miracle of self-worth comes to Rudolph when he takes action on behalf of his community; I suspect the shepherds also found themselves filling new roles in their community (even while they may have continued to be shepherds). They had learned that the ordinary will be forever filled with Divine glory.

We too can experience similar miracles amid the busyness of Christmas preparations, the relaxing days following the holiday, and our future plans for the New Year. When our eyes are opened, we see past exterior appearances. The domestic, the unlikeable, the unlovely, all become Divine.

Let us keep our senses open for wonder and beauty—and then share that beauty with those we meet.

TODAY'S CHRISTMAS PRACTICE

Today, we returned to the shepherds, focusing this time on the angelic visitation and the angels' hymn of praise. Pause now to reflect on Luke 2:8–15. Now, take a moment to consider the unexpected places where

God's glory may shine forth. Where do you need to open your senses to the wonder of life? Where do you need God's guiding light? Where do you see God's glory and encounter God's grace? And finally, how might you participate in the flow of grace and light?

A CHRISTMAS PRAYER

Christ, make me an instrument of your peace.
Let me embrace the outsider and outlier,
seeing gifts in unexpected places
and bringing forth light where others see darkness.
Remind me that I am enriched by others' successes
and blessed by others' happiness.
Help me see the gifts embedded
in my own and others' perceived limitations.
Ubuntu, I am because of you.
We are because of one another.

THE EIGHTH DAY OF CHRISTMAS

JANUARY 1

In the beginning was the Word,
and the Word was with God,
and the Word was God.
The Word was in the beginning with God.
All things came into being
through the Word,
and without the Word not one
thing came into being.
What has come into
being in him was life,
and the life was the
light of all people.

(John 1:1–4)

The Incarnation is cosmic, and it is also earthy and fleshly. God's Child is born in a stable, an outbuilding, houseless, poor, and powerless.

And Incarnation bursts forth in unexpected places, even when the most chaotic kids in town take over the annual Christmas pageant. In Barbara Robinson's Christmas tale, *The Best Christmas Pageant Ever,* the Horrible Herdmans show up in church because they heard there are cookies and cake. Six children, chaotic, undisciplined, unbathed, and street-smart, join the pageant and bully the other kids until the Herdmans get the best parts in the play. Everyone expects a disaster, including the recently drafted director.

But something unexpected happens. The Herdmans hear the Christmas story for the first time. They hear it without filters—the story of a vulnerable family just like their own, hungry and looking for a place to stay. Imogene Herdman, cast as Mary, embraces the part, and as the play ends, she tears up. Her brother, playing the part of one of the magi, presents the Holy Child with the ham from their welfare basket. The most unlikely children reveal the birth of Jesus in a way no one had expected, revealing the down-to-earth holiness of Jesus' birth. They make this "the best Christmas pageant ever."

John's Gospel also describes God's love affair with the Earth in all its diversity, chaos, and grittiness. God creates out of love, the love of a Divine Parent for a child, and the love of Mary and Joseph for their newborn. God is not aloof.

God's love, the Wisdom and Word of God Incarnate, shines forth from the shabby stable and illuminates every cell and soul. Creation is Christlike. While there are false gods aplenty, some taught in churches and political rallies, the only God worth following bears a human face, embodying and revealing Divine love.

God is love. That's why the world exists. Our vocation is to mirror that Child "of the Parent's love begotten."[5] "Those who abide in love abide in God, and God abides in them" (1 John 4:16).

TODAY'S CHRISTMAS PRACTICE

Pause and meditate on John 1:1–4. Consider the Divine Wisdom that brings forth the universe. Reflect on the reality that this same Wisdom inspires and guides your own spiritual adventures.

Now ask yourself: Where do you, like the Herdmans, need to hear the story of Jesus' birth "for the first time"? Are there areas of your life, regions of your heart, that the Good News of the Incarnation has not penetrated? How might you open your life and inner self more fully to the reality of the gospel? Describe to yourself (or write in your journal) how the light of this reality might change your life. How might it shape your actions and thoughts in new ways?

A CHRISTMAS PRAYER

God of the New Year,
you have called me to be a "light of the world."
You have challenged me to "let my light shine."
Let me see your light in dim places,
and let me be your light in surprising places.
I ask for your guidance to bring forth my gifts
and the gifts of others.

THE NINTH DAY OF CHRISTMAS

JANUARY 2

The light shines in the darkness and the darkness did not overtake it.

(John 1:5)

God is light and in God there is no darkness at all.

(1 John 1:5)

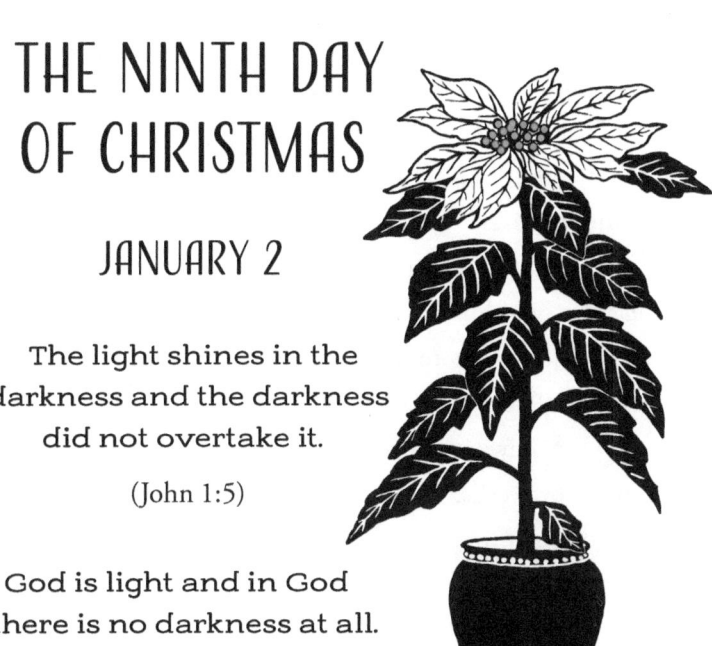

Christmas is about our inner spirit and not just the external trappings of parties and presents. This is the theme within Joanne Oppenheim and Fabian Negrin's children's book, *The Miracle of the First Poinsettia: A Mexican Christmas Story.* This folktale describes a Christmas miracle.

Christmas is not a happy time for Juanita and her family. Her father has lost his job, and there's no money for Christmas presents, nor can the family afford the celebrations of the nine days of Las Posadas.[6] Unlike last year when the family had a bountiful Christmas of gifts and treats, this year they have no money to buy even a simple basket of red berries to place on the altar as a gift to Baby Jesus at Midnight Mass.

Her hands empty, Juanita hides in the shadows outside the old church. Then, in the still night, she hears a sweet voice calling to her: "Juanita, you see the green leaves growing all around my wings?"

The only wings Juanita sees are carved on a stone angel hidden by weeds. "Pick the weeds," the angel encourages, "and don't worry how they will look. To the Baby Jesus they will not look like weeds. He will know they were a gift from your heart."

As Juanita walks down the aisle to present her gift at the altar, everyone in the church smiles in delight. The weeds she carries have been transformed into beautiful red flowers—*Floras de Noche Bene*, poinsettias.

When Juanita lays the flowers on the altar, she shares her heart with the Baby Jesus. "*Feliz Navidad, niño chiquito, Jesusito*," she says. (Merry Christmas, little baby Jesus.)

On the darkest night, the eye begins to see. Of course, darkness is not bad: it is the place of growth, birth, dreams, and rest. Still, the darkness where knowledge is lacking, where confusion reigns, where ignorance blocks the work of love, this is a cold darkness that stifles rather than births.

But God's love encompasses both the darkness of growth and the darkness of chaos. The Spirit brings to birth myriad possibilities and seeks always to heal the confusion that infects nations and persons. God lights the way in every instance, seeking health and vision in the chaos of our lives.

God is out to heal you, not harm you. Divinity's goal is love, not judgment. Let us walk in the light and love one another, as God has loved us.

TODAY'S CHRISTMAS PRACTICE

Reflect for a moment on the words of John 1:5 and 1 John 1:5. Imagine the power of light to transform chaos.

Now think about the "dark" areas in your own life, areas of confusion, apathy, or coldness. Imagine you hold a candle or perhaps the flashlight on your cell phone; as you hold it aloft in the cold and darkness, it casts just enough light to warm and illumine the steps

ahead. You cannot see the length of your path, but you see just enough to walk forward safely.

You might write one or both of today's scriptures on notecards and post them on your bathroom mirror, on a kitchen cupboard, on your desk or computer, and on your car's dashboard, anywhere you will see them throughout the day. Hold on to this scripture in your thoughts. It can be the "flashlight" you extend today to light your way.

Finally, consider the areas of your life and heart where can you already see this light at work in your life. How might you expand the light to reach further? What is getting in the way, casting "shadows" across your sense of yourself and your life? How might you become more transparent to the light of Christ's love, allowing it to shine through you and out into the world? Remind yourself throughout the day: You are a Light Carrier!

A CHRISTMAS PRAYER

I confess, O Jesus, that I am afraid of the dark.
I am afraid of the dark in the world and in myself.
I am afraid of what I see in the news.
I am afraid of demagogues in my nation,
the reality of climate change,
and its impact on the next generations.
I am afraid of sickness and growing older.
And yet the everlasting light
shines in the dim places of fear and hate.
The everlasting light cannot be quenched,
neither by my fears nor the machinations
of those who seek to destroy and divide.
Help me see your light,
even in people whose actions frighten me,
and give me courage to confront coldness with warmth,
confusion with illumination,
and fear with love.
Let the darkness in my life
be a place of love and growth,
rather than fear and anxiety.

THE TENTH DAY OF CHRISTMAS

JANUARY 3

The true light, which enlightens everyone,
was coming into the world....
But to all who received him,
who believed in his name,
he gave power to become children of God.

(John 1:9,12)

Don't you just love the sound of the word, "Grinch"? I recall my toddler son racing around the house forty years ago, shouting, "Grinch, Grinch, Grinch!" It's a word, like "Scrooge," whose sound somehow reflects its meaning: a tight-fisted killjoy, a party pooper, someone who hates other people having fun, someone who hates Christmas.

In Dr. Suess's tale, the Grinch loathes Christmas. What's worse, he hates the joy the Who's in Whoville get from celebrating Christmas.

Who knows why the Grinch is like this? Was it a childhood trauma? A disappointing Christmas in his past? Or has some other emotional condition rendered his heart two sizes too small? Whatever the cause of the Grinch's antipathy toward Christmas, he decides to finally put an end to Christmas joy in Whoville.

"I must find some way to stop Christmas from coming," the Grinch schemes. He dresses as Santa and takes all the trappings of Christmas—the presents, the food, the decorations, even the logs in the fireplace and the Christmas trees—from the houses of Whoville. "This will be the end of it," he gloats.

But then, instead of tears and wailing, he hears music: All the Who's are singing, despite the loss of all their Christmas trappings. In his astonishment at this merriment, the Grinch discovers the deeper meaning of Christmas. "Maybe Christmas doesn't come from a store. Maybe Christmas perhaps means a little bit more."

With that realization, the Grinch's heart grows three sizes. He returns all the gifts and decorations, and then, at the invitation of his new friends, he carves the roast beast!

Like Scrooge in Dicken's tale, the Grinch learns Christmas is about joy, not materialism, and he delights in his newfound community. The story concludes:

> Christmas Day will always be
> just as long as we have we.

As the first chapter of John's Gospel proclaims, God's light illumines everyone. Everyone! Friend and foe, neighbor and stranger, descendent of the pilgrims and child of undocumented workers. No one is excluded. The light is there for all to see, freely available, never denied to anyone.

And when we see this light, we receive the power of God's children. The power of love. The power of community. The power of healing. The power of a heart that grows three sizes.

God's light is in you and in all things. Rejoice!

TODAY'S CHRISTMAS PRACTICE

Take a moment to slowly read John 1:9–13. Are there any "Grinches" in your life, people who seem to cast shadows rather than shed light? How do these verses apply to individuals such as these? Can you see even a glimmer of Divine light in their lives?

Now reflect on what it might mean to have the power to become God's child. Can you sense your family connection to Divinity? Consider how God's power differs from our usual understandings of power. How would claiming God as your Parent energize and empower you?

A CHRISTMAS PRAYER

Loving God, keep my heart open.
Deliver me from a small spirit
and a cramped imagination.
Touch my heart that it might grow three sizes,
becoming big enough
to embrace the world you love.

THE ELEVENTH DAY OF CHRISTMAS

JANUARY 4

And the Word became flesh
and lived among us,
and we have seen his glory,
the glory as of a
father's only son,
full of grace and truth.

(John 1:14)

The film *Miracle on 34th Street*, another of my favorites, first came on the screen in 1947, telling a story about a replacement Santa Claus who reveals the miracles woven through ordinary life. When the store Santa arrives intoxicated at the annual

Macy's Thanksgiving Day Parade, Doris Walker hires Kris—a kindly man with a white beard—to be the store Santa. Susan soon comes to realize Kris not only plays Santa Claus; he also believes he *is* Santa Claus. Doris has taught her young daughter, Susan, not to believe in fairy tales like the existence of Santa Claus. Nevertheless, Susan comes to believe Kris is truly Santa.

In a comedy of errors, Kris is given a psychological evaluation, sent to Bellevue Hospital for observation, has a court hearing, and eventually is judged to be completely sane in his identification of himself as Santa Claus. Meanwhile, young Susan shows Kris a photo of her dream house; she tells Kris this house is her Christmas wish.

But when Christmas morning arrives, there is no dream house for Susan and Doris. Susan is crushed and once more doubts that Santa Claus is real.

Kris is unperturbed. He suggests that Fred, the next-door neighbor with whom Doris has begun a romantic relationship, drive Susan and Doris home by an alternate route to avoid traffic. On the way, Susan sees her dream house—and it has a "For Sale" sign posted in the front yard. Fred stops the car to investigate, and Susan runs into the house.

After the two adults follow her inside, Fred turns to Susan and proposes they get married and purchase the house. Then they notice something: Kris's cane is leaning against the wall by the fireplace. It dawns on them that Kris just might be the real thing—and miracles really do happen!

Divine miracles are everywhere when we have eyes to see—and Christmas is the season of miracles: unexpected moments and "thin places" where Heaven and Earth meet, weary hearts are healed, and skeptics discern it's a wonderful life. As Walt Whitman averred, "Every hour of the light and dark is a miracle, every cubic inch of space is a miracle."[7] William Blake, another mystic poet, proclaimed: "If the doors of perception were cleansed every thing would appear to humans as it is—Infinite. For human beings have closed themselves up, till they see all things thro' narrow chinks of their cavern."[8]

The philosopher Alfred North Whitehead says God is the fellow sufferer who understands and the joyful companion who celebrates. Divinity is with us at every moment of every day. "The Word became flesh," announces John's Gospel. Jesus bears human DNA! He is like us, and he is in us, as we are in him. Jesus is our kin. He feels our joys and sorrows, pleasure and pain, success and failure.

This is the same love Kris demonstrates in *A Miracle on 34th Street*. A child's wistful longing; a woman's skeptical, wounded heart; and crowds seeking the true meaning of

Christmas among the holiday rush—Kris notices and has compassion on them all. What's more, he reaches out with practical advice that creates genuine miracles in the lives of everyone with whom he interacts.

During Jesus' earthly life, he too noticed the pain of those around him—and he too reached out with practical help to nourish and heal. No person was too small, too insignificant, too despicable; Divine love lifted them all.

More than two thousand years after Jesus' birth in Bethlehem, the miracle of his Being continues to interpenetrate our lives. His face is imprinted on ours, and he mirrors our faces in all our uniqueness and diversity. God is in the child in Gaza and Israel. Divinity is the inner-city teen, the suburban middle schooler, the university professor, the undocumented worker, the social justice activist, and the MAGA supporter. All around us, the Word is made flesh! God is in our cells and souls, inviting us to see and claim the miracle of the Divine Presence everywhere.

TODAY'S CHRISTMAS PRACTICE

Read John 1:14 again. Take a moment to sit with this verse, allowing its words to form images and ideas in your head. Make a list of anything that comes to mind; there are no wrong answers!

Now imagine the Divinity that shines in your flesh and blood. Picture your skin, your bones, your muscles, your very cells glowing with God's light—and know this is a reality, not just your imagination (even if it's not visible to human eyes). Next, see that same light shining from bodies of all kinds: black, white, and brown; nonbinary, female, transgender, and male; human and nonhuman, animal life and plant life; babies, teenagers, adults, and elders; neurodiverse individuals and neurotypical; athletes and couch potatoes; thin folk and overweight ones; people whose bodies have limitations and those who don't. Each body, each cell, each atom and subatomic particle rejoices in the wondrous diversity of God's artistry.

A CHRISTMAS PRAYER

I thank you, Life-Giver, for the wonder of my being.
I thank you for the miracle of flesh and blood,
even when I feel the aches and pains of normal life.
I thank you for my senses;
sharpen them so I might see
the miracles all around me.
Make me always ready
to see the world's beauty, to smell the aroma
of pine needles and cookies baking,
to feel the skin of a loved one,
to taste sweetness and spice in
Christmas pudding and pies,
and hear the melodies of carols and hymns.
Let me live in gratitude for these miracles—
and may my gratitude energize me
to build a world where everyone has all they need
for health, for growth, for joy.

THE TWELFTH DAY OF CHRISTMAS

JANUARY 5

On coming to the house,
[the magi] saw the child with
his mother Mary,
and they bowed down and worshipped him.
Then they opened their treasures
and presented him
with gifts of gold, frankincense and myrrh.

(Matthew 2:11)

"One dollar and eighty-seven cents." So begins O'Henry's short story "The Gift of the Magi." It's the day before Christmas, and Della doesn't have a gift for her husband James. She dreams of getting a chain for his prized gold watch, but she doesn't have enough money. Meanwhile, James is also ruminating on how to give Della the perfect gift with his modest salary; he wants to buy expensive combs for her beautiful hair.

Starting in the 1940s, the Hallmark company's slogan for its cards was "when you care enough to send the very best." This is what both Della and James want for the other: the very best. Della sells her hair to buy a watch chain for James. James sells his gold watch to purchase combs for Della's glorious hair. Oh, the irony!

And yet the story ends with an affirmation of Della and James' foolish and loving wisdom.

> The magi, as you know, were wise men—wonderfully wise men—who brought gifts to the newborn Christ-child. They were the first to give Christmas gifts. Being wise, their gifts were doubtless wise ones. And here I have told you the story of two children who were not wise. Each sold the most valuable thing he owned in order to buy a gift for the other. But let me speak a last word to the wise of these days: Of all who give gifts, these two were the most wise. Of all who give and receive gifts, such as they are the most wise. Everywhere they are the wise ones. They are the magi.

This is the foolish power of love, which goes beyond the calculating love of privilege and control.

Scripture says that magi from the East visited the Child Jesus. They came to pay homage to the "king of the Jews" with gifts of gold, frankincense, and myrrh—amazing treasures for a peasant child! I wonder what Mary and Joseph did with these gifts. Did they sell them to support their growing family? Did they give them away to someone else in need? Or did Mary put them away in a safe corner to bring out and show Jesus as he grew older, a reminder of his identity? I wonder if Mary wished for gifts that were a bit more practical, such as food, diapers, clothing. And yet I'm sure she knew, as Della and James did, that the greatest gift is always love.

The magi may have had the personal wealth to easily purchase the gifts they brought, but their sacrifice lay in the long and dangerous journey they made to seek the Child; this was the demonstration of their love. These Zoroastrian spiritual leaders sought God's light in another religious tradition, in a place where they were considered outsiders, culturally, ethnically, and religiously.

Including this story in the Christmas narrative reminds us that spiritual insight is broadcast universally. God's wisdom, in whom we "live and move and have our being" (Acts 17:28), is bestowed upon every person, regardless of religion, ethnicity, economics, citizenship, age, or sexuality. The birth of Jesus is larger than any faith tradition, culture, or class. Even the stars give homage to God's Beloved Child. "Heaven and nature sing," and "all nature sings and around me rings the music of the spheres."[9]

Like Della and James' love, Divine love sacrifices to bring joy to the world. In the wondrous miracle of Christmas, Divinity gives the very best, God's beloved Child. Amazed by God's bountiful revelation, we, like the magi of old, like James and Della, share our gifts for the Christ Child at Christmas, as well as all year long.

From the perspective of our materialist world, love may seem foolish. What use are combs when your hair is short? What good is a watch chain when the watch is gone? How will a baby born into a poor family have use for exotic treasures? But love doesn't mind looking foolish, and it is willing to take risks in order to express itself. Love is made real in the work we do for the Realm of Heaven, the sacrifices we make for those we love, and the effort we take to bring delight to others. As Madeleine L'Engle wrote:

> This is no time for a child to be born,
> With the earth betrayed by war and hate. . . .
> Yet Love still takes the risk of birth.[10]

TODAY'S CHRISTMAS PRACTICE

Take a few moments now to read Matthew 2:1–12, reflecting on the words and images that speak most to you. Imagine yourself at the Nativity; what gifts would you bring the Christ Child?

As you go through the day, think about your actions as potential gifts to the Christ Child. How might you be more attentive to the face of Jesus in the forgotten, vulnerable, and oppressed? Even the smallest gift—a smile, a kind word, a helping hand—can change a life and transform the world. Don't let embarrassment or shyness (the fear of looking foolish) hold you back. Be willing to take a risk!

A CHRISTMAS PRAYER

Loving God, let me live by abundance.
Let my life be full of love and possibility.
Let my heart and hands be open to others.
Let my life be a gift to you and those around me.

THE FEAST OF EPIPHANY

JANUARY 6

> And having been warned in a dream
> not to return to Herod,
> they left for their own country
> by another road.
>
> (Matthew 2:12)

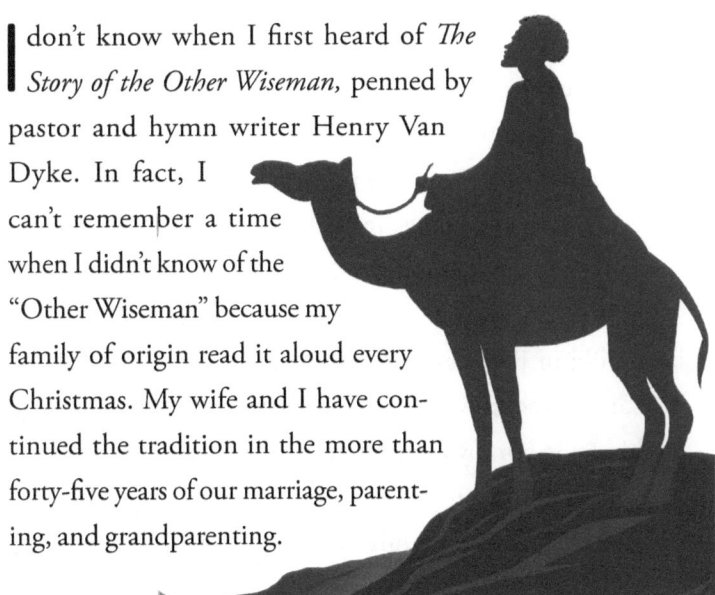

I don't know when I first heard of *The Story of the Other Wiseman,* penned by pastor and hymn writer Henry Van Dyke. In fact, I can't remember a time when I didn't know of the "Other Wiseman" because my family of origin read it aloud every Christmas. My wife and I have continued the tradition in the more than forty-five years of our marriage, parenting, and grandparenting.

The story joins time and eternity, demonstrating that Divine revelation shines on the unexpected roads not taken. It is a story that never grows old. On a long, lonely night, in a time fraught with personal anguish, the Fourth Wiseman came to the author Henry van Dyke as a "gift. "It was sent to me," he wrote. "It seemed as if I knew the giver, though His name was not spoken."

Artaban, a Persian magus, goes in search of the Child, following the star of Bethlehem, carrying three precious stones: a sapphire, a ruby, and a pearl. He intends to meet his companion magi to travel together to worship the Promised Child, but along his way, a wounded man stops him. He provides aid but misses the connection with his friends.

Short on funds now, he sells his sapphire to finance his lonely journey to Bethlehem. But he arrives three days too late. Once again, he has missed his companions, and the Holy Family has fled to Egypt.

While Artaban is sharing a meal with a young mother and child in Bethlehem, the Roman legions storm the village, intent on killing every child. Artaban saves the young child beside him by exchanging his ruby for the child's life.

Next, Artaban travels south, seeking the Child in Egypt. Once again, he misses out, but he spends the next thirty-three years serving the poor of Egypt. Finally, still searching for the Holy Child, Artaban arrives in Jerusalem, just in time for Jesus' crucifixion. He hopes to save Christ's life by bribing the Romans with the "pearl of great price" he still carries with him. As he hurries to the Roman headquarters, however, he is confronted by another person in need; he spends his last treasure to ransom a young woman from being sold into slavery.

No longer in possession of any treasures, Artaban knows he has failed in his quest. And yet he feels at peace. "He knows that all is well, because he had done the best that he could, from day to day. He had been true to the light that had been given him."

Then the earth quakes, and Artaban is struck by a falling tile. As he dies, he encounters the Christ and confesses his failure to help him—but Jesus honors his quest. A voice tells him, in the spirit of Matthew 25:31–46, "Verily I say unto thee, inasmuch as thou hast done it unto one of the least of these my brethren, thou hast done it unto me." Although Artaban thought he was a failure, he discovers he encountered the Christ on every step of his journey.

With the best of intentions, we make plans for our lives. Sometimes—often times—our lives turn out completely different from what we had imagined. The Other

Wise Man never reaches the Christ Child. Thanks to Herod's violence and hatred, his friends, the other magi, take another road home from the one they had planned.

When we fail to achieve our goals, we, like Artaban, might feel like failures. But twists and turns on life's path need not be negative. Often our life changes course as a result of a new insight that renders our previous plans irrelevant and obsolete. Other times, an unexpected event—a synchronous encounter, an inspiring book, a mystical experience, a brush with death through illness or accident, a job loss, or even a death—changes the course of our lives.

Such moments are overwhelming and unsettling. They can also be exhilarating and exciting. With new routes come new adventures and unplanned risks—but like Artaban, we may discover a fellow Adventurer has been with us all along. This Companion guides us on a Holy Adventure, transforming our lives and the world around us.

TODAY'S CHRISTMAS PRACTICE

Read Matthew 2:12 again, meditating on the phrases and words. Ponder your own roads not taken. Do these lost pathways still hurt your heart? Or have you released them to God, accepting that the Divine has a different route planned for you?

Now consider what new paths you may be called to take between now and next Christmas. Does anything tug at your heart? In the days ahead, continue to reflect on this question. Pray to see more clearly what God has in mind. Are there plans you might need to abandon in order to be faithful to God's dreams for your life?

A CHRISTMAS PRAYER

Let this day be truly an epiphany.
Let me see you, Christ,
revealed in all things
and experience your grace
on every path I take.
Let every pathway,
even the unexpected ones,
guide me to you.
And may every day in the year ahead
be Christmas, a day on which
you are born into the world.

NOTES

1. Alfred North Whitehead, *Adventures of Ideas* (New York: Free Press, 1967), 167.

2. Whitehead, *Process and Reality: Corrected Edition* (New York: Free Press), 342.

3. December 28 is remembered as the Feast of the Holy Innocents in the Western church, while Eastern Orthodox congregations celebrate it on December 29, as I have chosen to do. Branches of the Syrian Christian church also celebrate this feast on both December 27 and January 10.

4. Found in *A Treasury of African American Christmas Stories,* compiled and edited by Bettye Collier Thomas (Boston: Beacon Press, 2018), 202–211.

5. Marcus Aurelius Clemens Prudentius, "Of the Parent's Heart Begotten" (fourth century).

6. Las Posadas is a religious festival celebrated in Mexico and some parts of the United States between

December 16th and 24th. It commemorates Joseph and Mary's journey from Nazareth to Bethlehem and their search for a safe refuge where Mary can give birth to the Baby Jesus.

7. Walt Whitman, "Miracles," *World Literature* (Quezon City, Philippines: Katha Publishing, 2000), 14.

8. William Blake, *The Marriage of Heaven and Hell*, quoted in *Blake and Tradition, Volume II* by Kathleen Raine (New York: Routledge, 2002), 108. Blake's original words have been slightly changed to allow for gender inclusivity.

9. Isaac Watts, "Joy to the World" (1719), and Maltbie Babcock, "This is My Father's World" (1901).

10. Madeleine L'Engle, "The Risk of Birth," *The Ordering of Love: The New and Collected Poems of Madeleine L'Engle* (New York: Random House, 2009), 155.

More inspiration for
the Christmas season...

THE WORK OF CHRISTMAS
The 12 Days of Christmas with Howard Thurman

This book is a celebration of the twelve days of Christmas, offering us a chance to dwell on the meaning of the season in dialogue with the wisdom of one of America's greatest mystics and activists, Howard Thurman.

During the twelve days of Christmas, our goal is to experience God's light, despite the temptation to close our hearts in a world too often characterized by racism, sexism, polarization, nationalism, and exclusion. This season asks us instead to open our hearts and our lives, so that throughout the year ahead, we may be light-bearers, carrying the message of Divine justice and hope, making it come alive even in the darkest corners of the world. This is the year-round work of Christmas!

I WONDER AS I WANDER
The 12 Days of Christmas with Madeleine L'Engle

How can we recover the radical meaning of the Christmas season? Using the thoughts and words of Madeleine L'Engle, this books offers you a guide through the hectic Christmas season. With quiet times of prayer, Scripture, and meditation, you can begin to wonder—to imagine big possibilities and ask important questions—as you wander outside your typical comfort zones. In the twelve days of Christmas, bookended by Christmas Eve and the Feast of Epiphany, you will experience anew the awe and wonder of the Incarnation.

As you both wonder and wander, the questions and images in this book will open your heart to the radical message of Christmas.

THIN PLACES EVERYWHERE
The 12 Days of Christmas with Celtic Christianity

Bruce Epperly invites you to share a Christmas adventure with him, voyaging through the 12 days of Christmas (plus Christmas Eve and Epiphany) with Brendan, Columba, Brigid, Patrick, and other Celtic saints. With these Celtic adventurers as your companions, you will discover "thin places"—moments of time when the Incarnation of Christ shines through ordinary people, places, and events. After the busyness of Advent, the days that follow Christmas can be a quieter time, when you can venture out on an inner vision quest for new ways of seeing and being. May your Christmas journey awaken you to thin places everywhere.

REPAIRING THE WORLD
The 12 Days of Christmas with Francis & Clare of Assisi

During the Twelve Days of Christmas, Clare and her spiritual companion Francis ask us to consider the following questions:

- Where do I see Christ in my life and the world?
- What clutters my life, spiritually and physically?
- What one action can I take to simplify my life in order to protect the environment and promote the well-being of others?

In the lull after Christmas Day, join Bruce, Francis, and Clare on their quest to repair the world, taking you beyond presents and parties to world loyalty and holy restlessness.

PRAYING TWICE
The 12 Days of Christmas with Carols and Hymns

In our Christmas carols, we find praise, contemplation, lamentation, and affirmation. Singing them, we join the angelic chorus with the shepherds, participating in the harmonies of the spheres. Our carols rise to the heavens and plumb the unconscious depths of the Spirit, where the "sighs too deep for words" whisper.

This holiday season, extend the Christmas joy through the traditional twelve days that lead up to Epiphany. Celebrate each day with Bruce Epperly, meditating on the familiar words of Christmas carols. Sing and pray at the same time, as you rejoice in the coming of Love and Wisdom into our world, embodied in a Child whose compassionate embrace is greater than any challenge.

SANTA CLAUS
Saint, Shaman, & Symbol

If you don't believe in Santa, you might want to reconsider. The familiar fellow dressed in red has been around a lot longer than the malls' Santa, longer than Rudolph, longer even than "The Night Before Christmas." His earliest and most ancient forms brought hope and cheer to generation after generation of humankind—and he still has a message for us today. In the midst of the materialism of the modern holiday, Santa offers us a bridge between the physical, secular world and the spiritual, sacred realm. Discover his history and evolution, from Ice Age shaman to medieval saint to modern-day icon. Get to know Santa—and believe all over again.

Prepare the Way
Celtic Prayers for the Season of Light

Ray Simpson has given his life, both professionally and personally, to Celtic Christianity, and now he helps us to celebrate a Celtic outlook on the season of Christmas. With their eloquent yet simple words, his prayers welcome the Holy One who comes to us in small, ordinary ways, who is present in the helpless and the vulnerable. As we join Ray in prayer, we stand on the threshold to paradox and mystery—and we "prepare the way" for God to enter our world anew.

BRUCE G. EPPERLY has served as a seminary professor and administrator, university chaplain, and congregational pastor. An ordained minister with the United Church of Christ and Christian Church (Disciples of Christ), he is the author of more than sixty books, including *From Cosmos to Cradle: Meditations on the Incarnation*; *Jesus: Mystic, Healer, and Prophet;* and *Homegrown Mystics: Restoring Our Nation with the Healing Wisdom of America's Visionaries.*

AnamcharaBooks.com

www.ingramcontent.com/pod-product-compliance
Lightning Source LLC
Chambersburg PA
CBHW060532080526
44586CB00012B/709